LEARN TO DRAW

Disney

PLANES

Featuring Dusty Crophopper, Skipper Riley, Ripslinger, El Chupacabra, and all your favorite characters!

Walter Foster

3 5 7 9 10 8 6 4 2

CONTENTS

THE STORY OF

Disney

PLANES

Dusty Crophopper spends his days above Propwash Junction, Minnesota, spraying the fields with Vitaminamulch, but at the end of every workday, the little crop duster pursues his true passion of air racing. His goal is to compete in the Wings Around The Globe Rally with the fastest racing planes in the world! His best friend, Chug, a fuel truck, helps train him until it becomes clear that Dusty needs a coach who has flying experience. Chug suggests Skipper, a gruff old navy warplane, but Dusty is less than enthusiastic. Skipper doesn't even fly anymore! When Dusty finally asks Skipper to coach him, the veteran flatly refuses. Undaunted, Dusty heads off to a qualifying race for the rally in Lincoln, Nebraska, with Chug and Dottie (Propwash Junction's ace mechanic) along for help and support.

At the race, Dusty is thrilled to see Ripslinger, his racing idol and a three-time Wings Around The Globe Rally winner. Rip, however, quickly reveals himself to be arrogant and mean-spirited. He makes fun of Dusty, and the crowd follows suit. Then, to everyone's surprise, Dusty flies amazingly well—and even comes close to qualifying for the rally. Dusty doesn't care that he held his own against actual racing planes; all he knows is that his time isn't good enough to get him into the rally. He returns home, hopes dashed, and vows to give up racing. Then, in a surprise turn of events, another racer is disqualified for cheating, and Dusty is given his spot in the rally! Finally a reluctant Skipper agrees to coach Dusty and soon discovers a problem: Dusty is afraid of heights. Flying low to dust the crops is no problem, but in racing, the most powerful tailwinds are at higher altitudes. Skipper puts Dusty through intensive training, and Dusty improves so much that by the time the rally rolls around, Skipper feels that the rookie might just be up to the challenge.

Dusty flies to JFK International Airport in New York, where the first leg of the rally will begin. When he joins the other racers on pit row, he is taken aback by how unwelcoming and competitive everyone is. The only two racers who are friendly to him are El Chupacabra, a masked racer from Mexico, and Ishani, a racing plane from India.

Despite a rocky start, Dusty perseveres with advice from Skipper, who entertains him with tales of his many navy missions. As the race goes on, Dusty becomes a hero to working vehicles everywhere who, like him, dream of doing more than they were built for. Though Ripslinger grows jealous of Dusty's newfound popularity and tries to thwart him at every turn, Dusty gains confidence, skill, and the respect of his competitors. As the racers fly around the globe facing dangerous

terrain and punishing weather, Dusty continues to fly low. It occasionally works to his advantage, but Skipper reminds his student that he must fly higher if he's to have a fighting chance against the other racers.

Dusty's prospects take a downward turn on the second-to-last leg of the race when one of Ripslinger's teammates breaks off Dusty's antenna. Dusty flies aimlessly until, just as he is about to run out of fuel, he is saved by two navy fighter jets. They escort him back to their ship, which happens to be Skipper's old aircraft carrier. There, Dusty learns that Skipper only flew one mission in his entire navy career. Refueled, repaired, and on his way to Mexico, Dusty tries to make sense of this startling discovery—and is caught in a violent storm! Because Dusty is still flying low, a wave crashes over him and drenches his engine. He sputters and crashes into the sea, where a Mexican navy helicopter rescues him.

When he is delivered to his friends, bruised and battered, Dusty's main concern is finding out why Skipper has been lying to him. Now his coach tells Dusty his big secret: As a young flying instructor, he lost his entire squadron of students on his very first mission. After that, he couldn't bring himself to fly again. Dusty doesn't know what to say. As he grapples with Skipper's betrayal, he must also face the fact that his dream is at an end. He is too damaged to fly in the final leg of the rally.

Just when things seem hopeless, his competitors—now his friends—each contribute new parts to replace Dusty's broken ones. With the help of the other racers' mechanics, Dottie works through the night to make Dusty good as new. Dusty takes off for the final leg with newfound confidence. But soon Ripslinger and his teammates close in and try to take Dusty out of the race. That's when Skipper comes roaring to the rescue—at last overcoming his own fear of flying and inspiring Dusty to confront his fear of heights. Dusty finally climbs high into the sky, catching the tailwinds he needs to win the rally! Skipper learns it's never too late to become a true hero, and Dusty becomes the racer he always dreamed he could be.

TOOLS & MATERIALS

Before you begin, gather some drawing tools, such as paper, a regular pencil, an eraser, and a pencil sharpener. For color, you can use markers, colored pencils, crayons, or even paint!

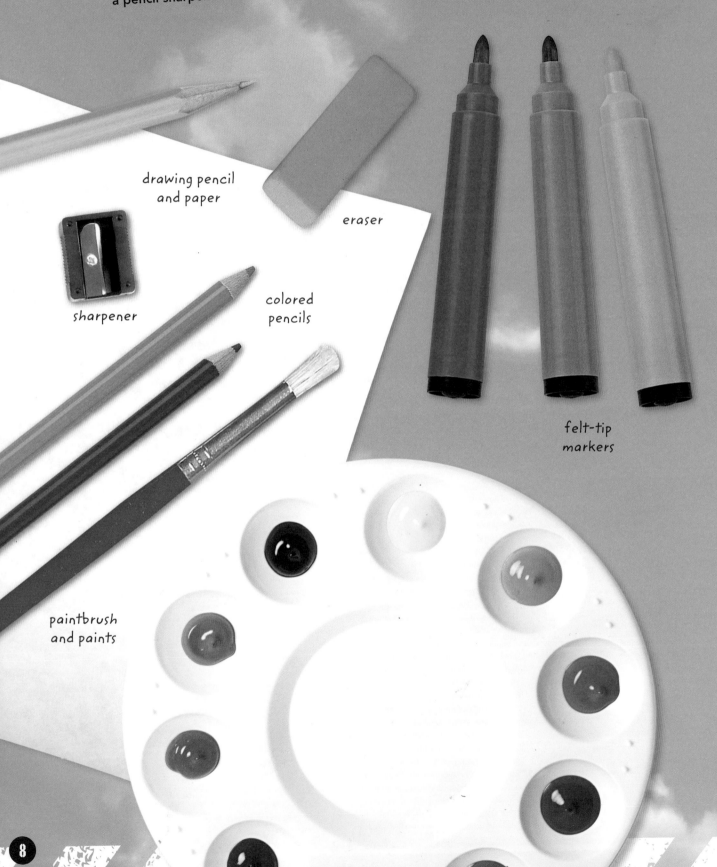

drawing pencil
and paper

eraser

sharpener

colored
pencils

felt-tip
markers

paintbrush
and paints

GETTING STARTED

Follow the steps shown below, and you will be
drawing Dusty and his high-flying friends in no time!

1

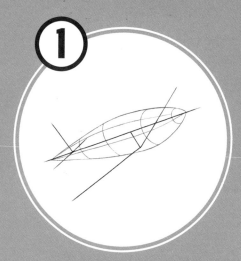

First draw basic shapes
using light lines that will
be easy to erase.

2

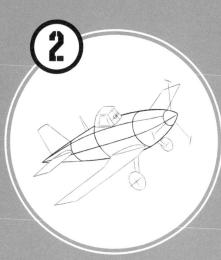

Each new step is shown in
blue, so you'll know what
to add next.

3

Follow the blue lines to
draw the details.

4

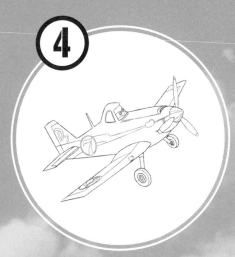

Now darken the lines
you want to keep, and
erase the rest.

5

Use some crayons or
markers to add color to
your drawing!

DRAWING EXERCISES

Warm up your hand by drawing squiggles and shapes on a piece of scrap paper.

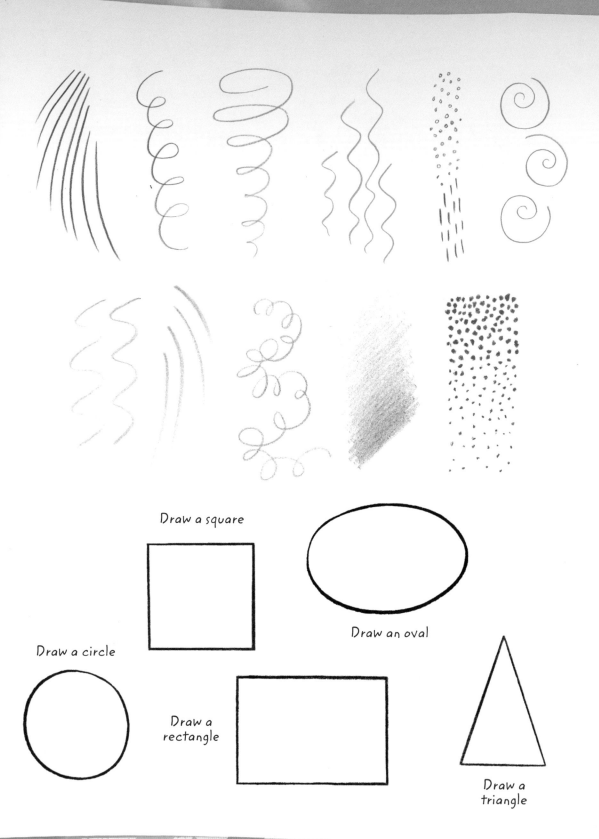

Draw a square

Draw an oval

Draw a circle

Draw a rectangle

Draw a triangle

Circle

Ball

Triangle

Ice cream cone

Pizza

Sun

Square

Gift

House

Rectangle

Book

Oval

Balloon

Submarine

Truck

DUSTY CROPHOPPER

Dusty is a plane with high hopes—literally. He sees himself soaring alongside his high-flying heroes in an international race. The fact that he's not really built for competitive racing doesn't stop him from pursuing his dream—but his fear of heights just might. With a little help from his friends, Dusty takes off on an adventure of a lifetime, daring to reach heights he never imagined possible.

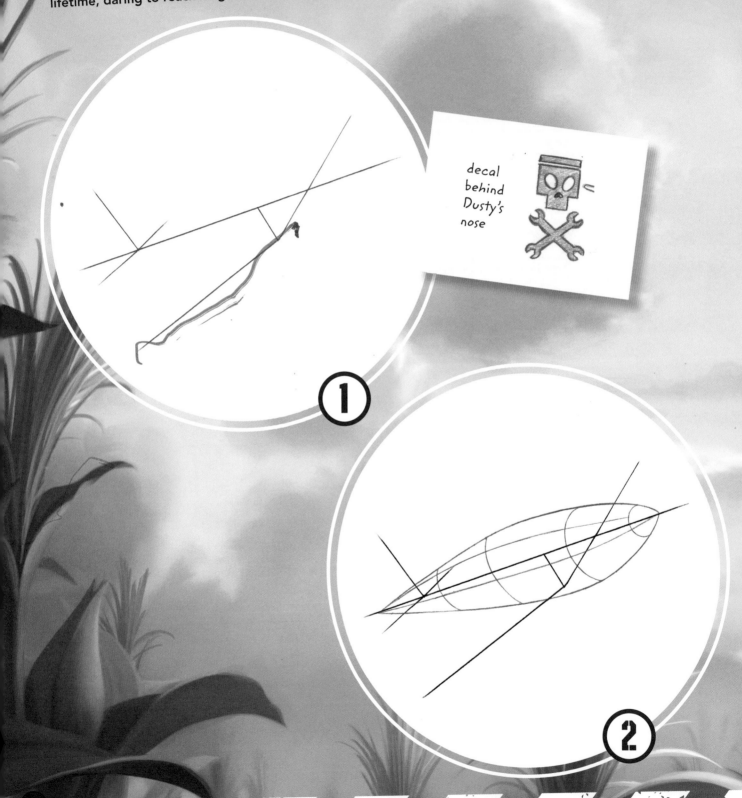

decal behind Dusty's nose

①

②

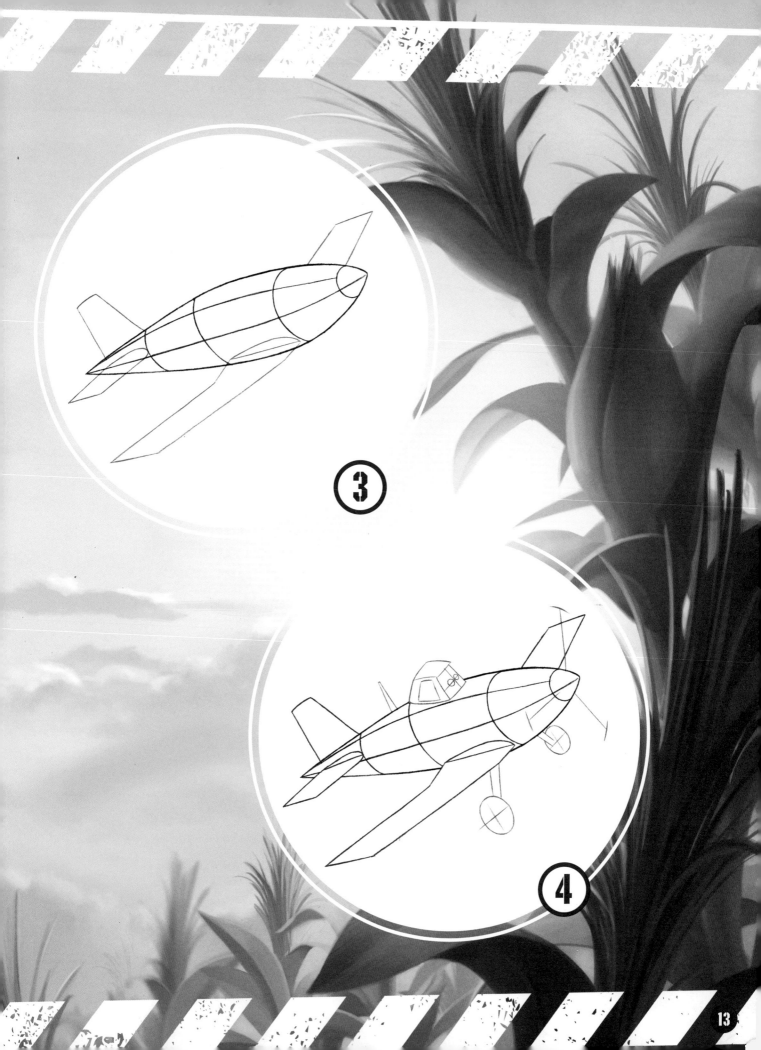

③

④

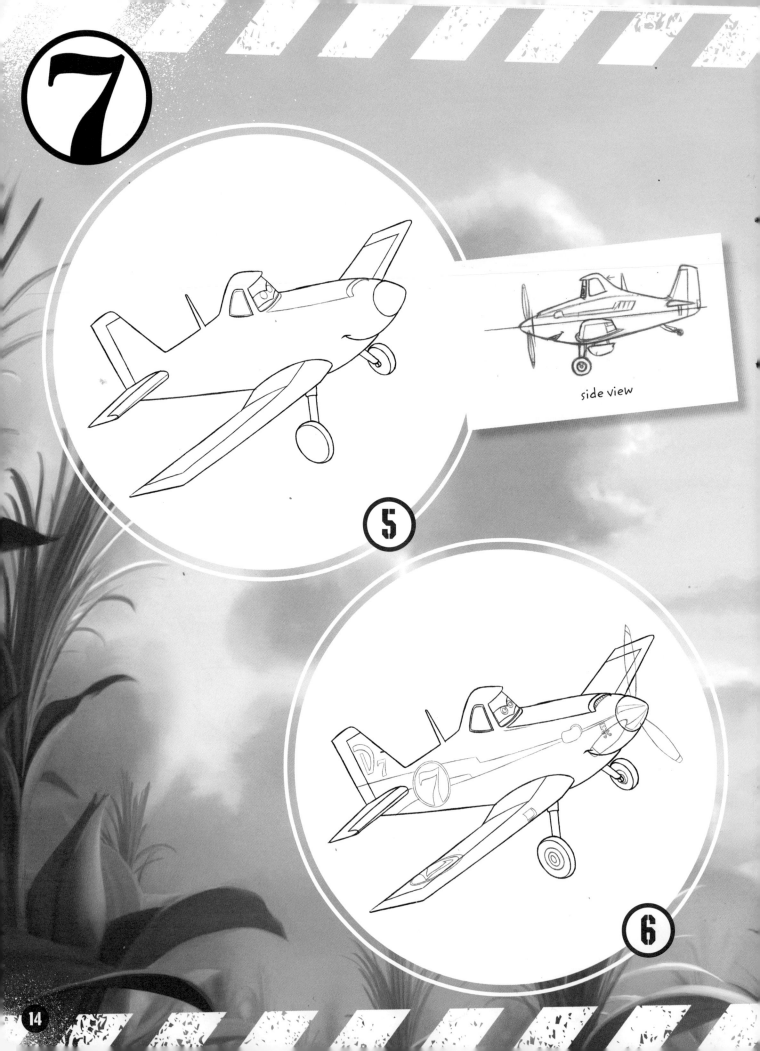

side view

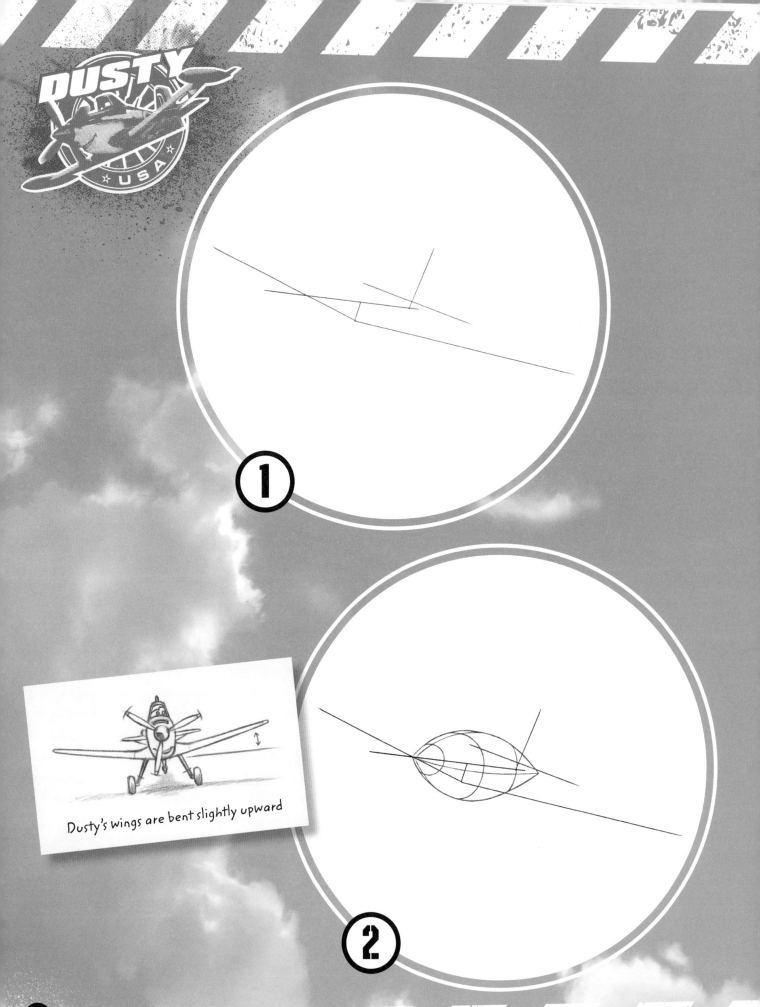

Dusty's wings are bent slightly upward

① ②

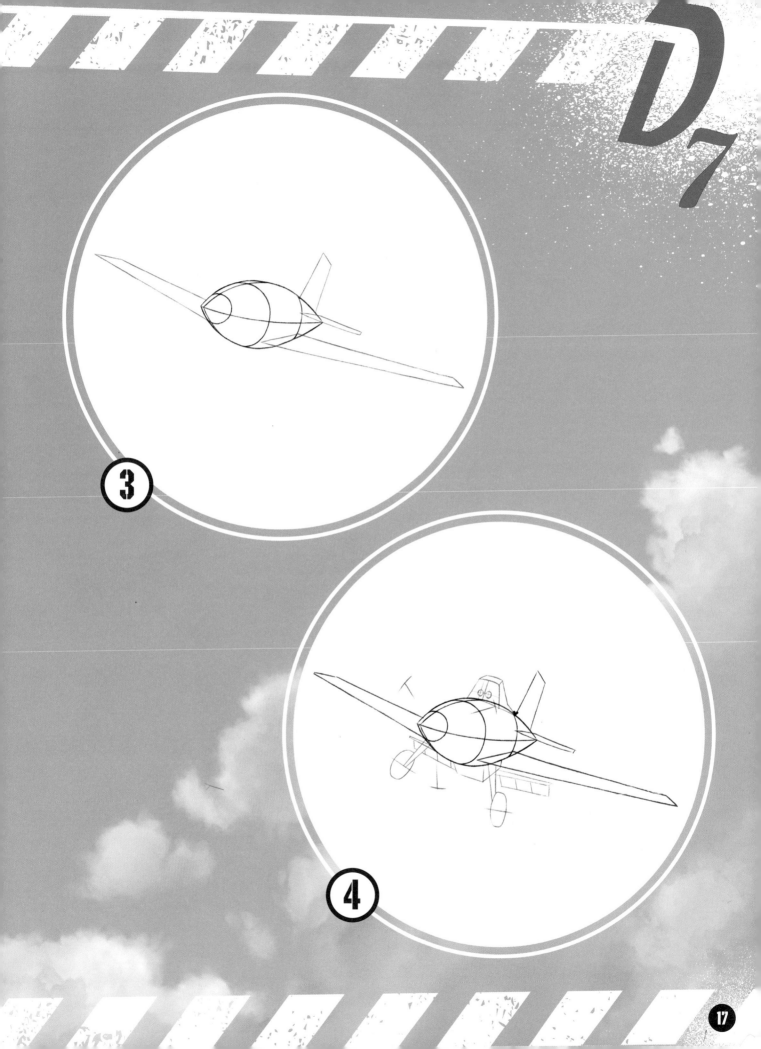

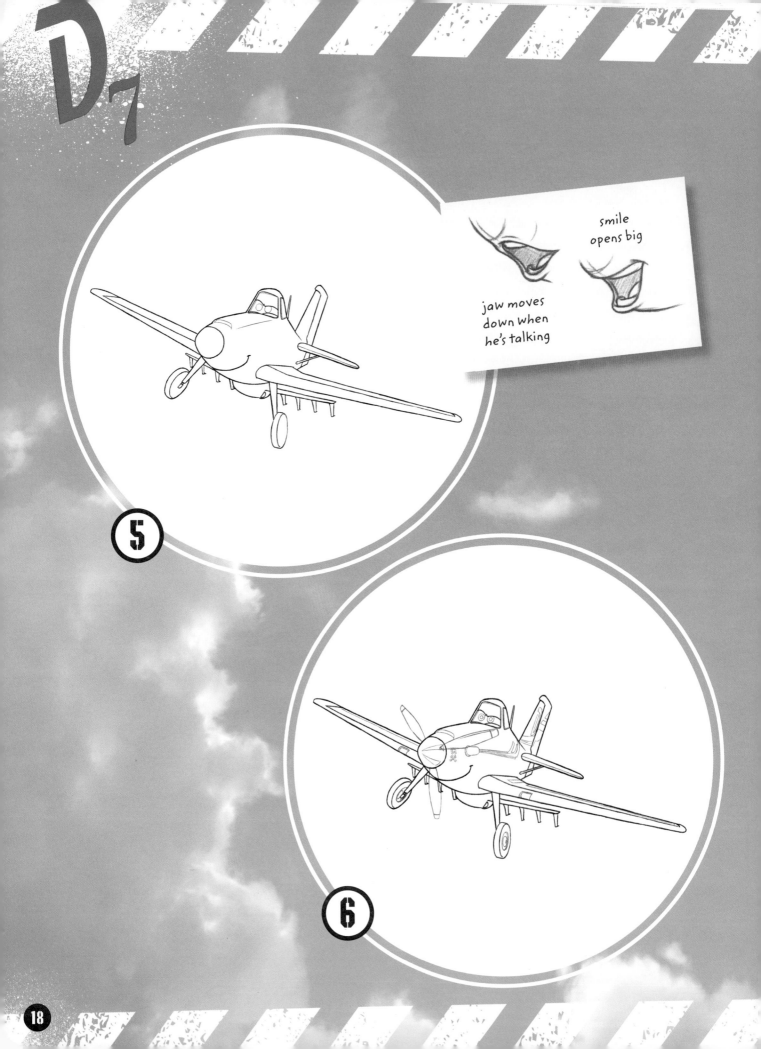

NO STOP!

7

YES!
straight lines
for wings

NO!
wings not
floppy

8

SKIPPER RILEY

A retired old Navy warplane, Skipper was an ace flier and top instructor of the esteemed Jolly Wrenches squadron until an incident during combat left him grounded for life. These days Skipper keeps to himself, but his quiet existence is turned upside down when Dusty asks for his aerial expertise—and gets a few life lessons in the process. While coaching Dusty, Skipper finds that he also has a few things to learn.

①

②

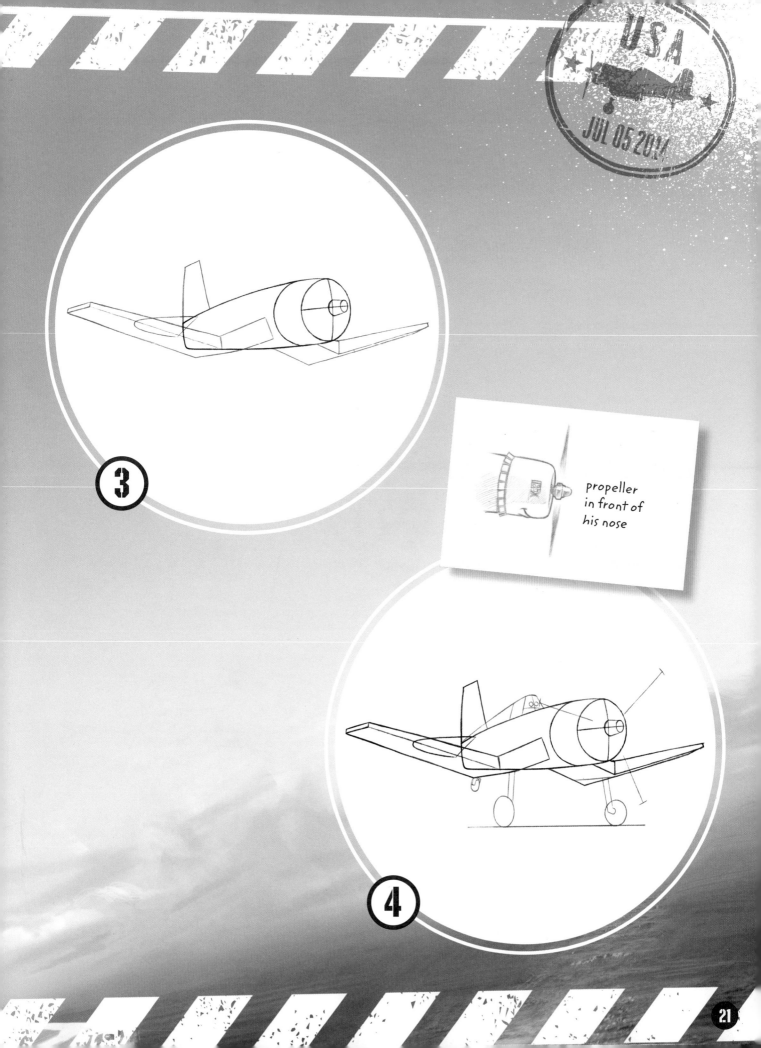

③

propeller
in front of
his nose

④

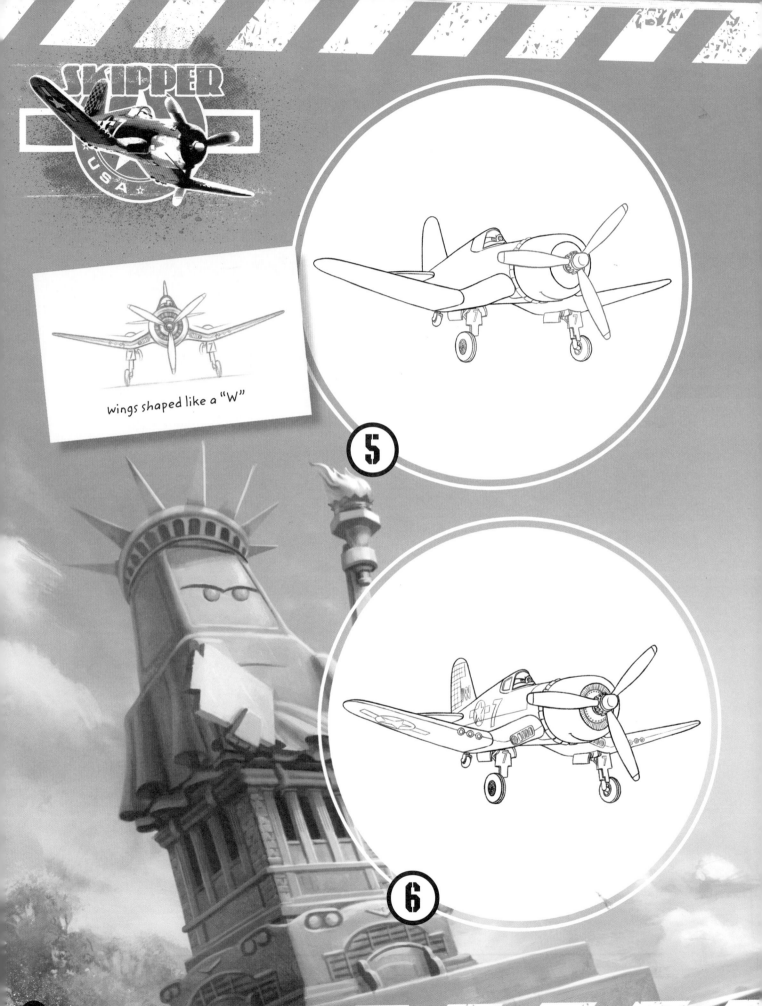

SKIPPER

USA

wings shaped like a "W"

5

6

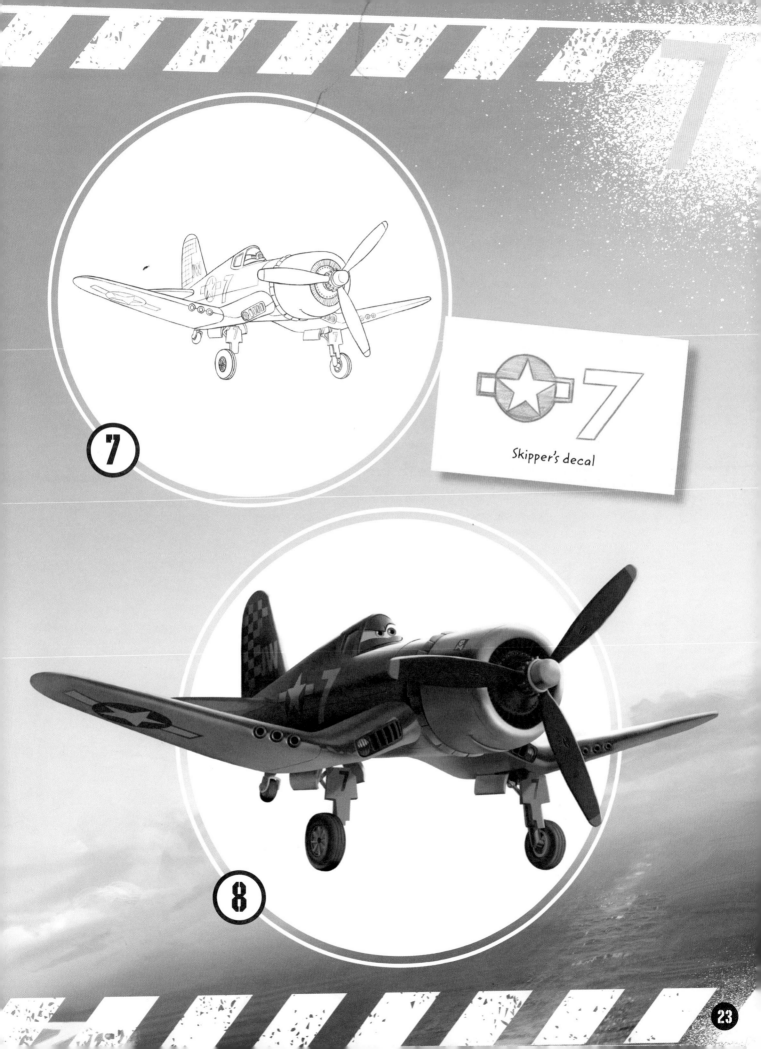

7

Skipper's decal

8

EL CHUPACABRA

The extremely charming El Chupacabra is a legend in Mexico (Just ask him!) Powered by his passion for racing, this champ is anything but low key—his booming voice and charismatic presence are as big as his oversized engine. No one really knows what is truth and what is delusion when it comes to El Chu, but one thing is beyond doubt: He races with a whole lot of heart and more dramatic flair than is recommended at high altitudes.

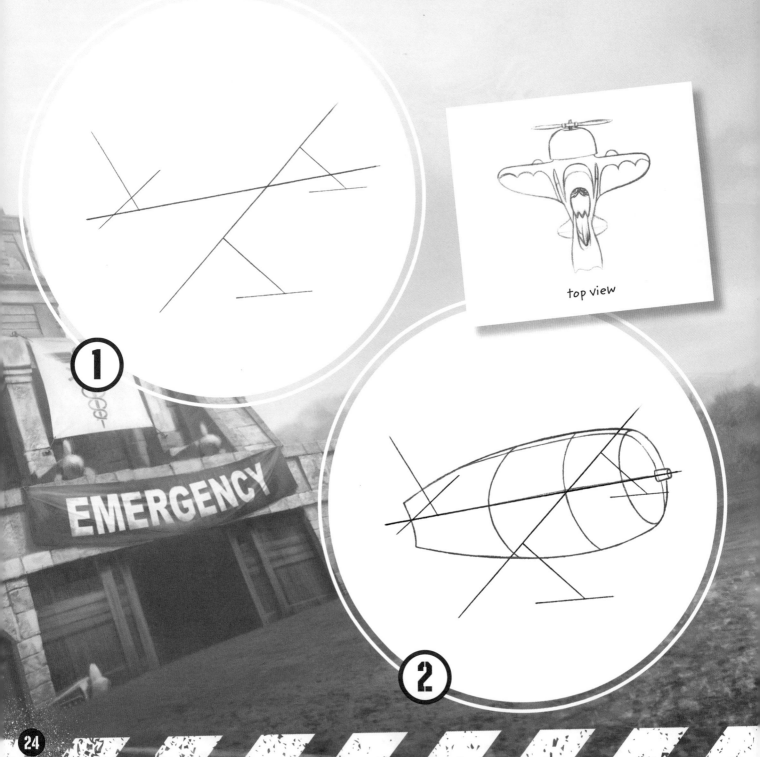

top view

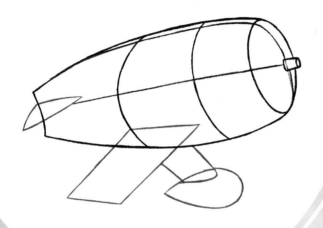

③

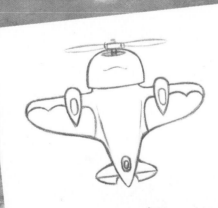

bottom view

④

MEXICO ★ 5 ★

El CHUPACABRA

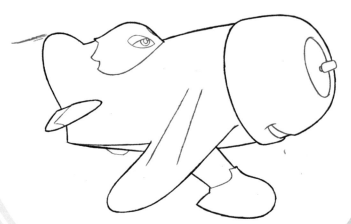

⑤

El Chu wears a mask

⑥

⑦

decal shows he
is número cinco
(number five)

⑧

RiPSLiNGER

With more wins than he can count, and just as many fans, Ripslinger is wings-down the biggest name in air racing—and he knows it. But even with the best funding and equipment, the three-time world champion still doesn't play fair—especially when it comes to a small-town plane with zero racing experience. Dusty doesn't belong in Ripslinger's sport, and this pro will do anything to take the new guy out of the race.

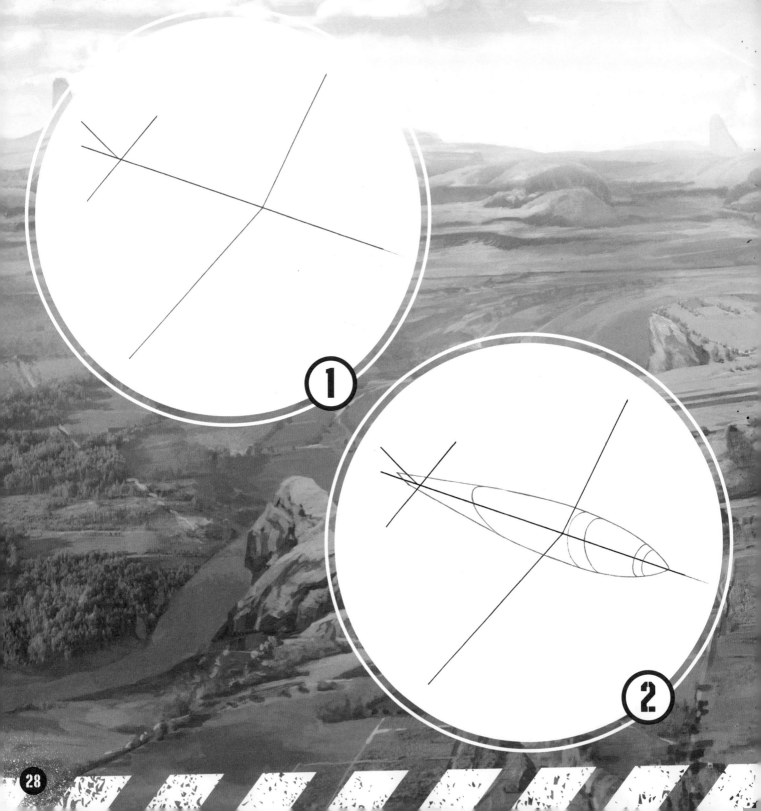

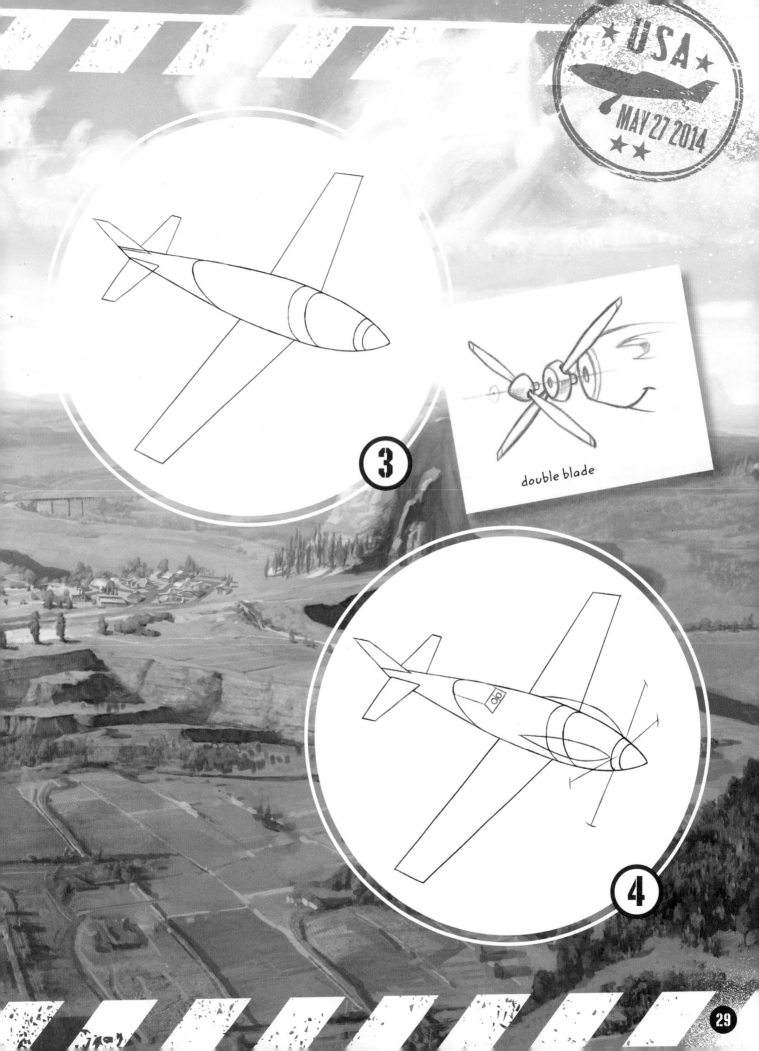

double blade

③

④

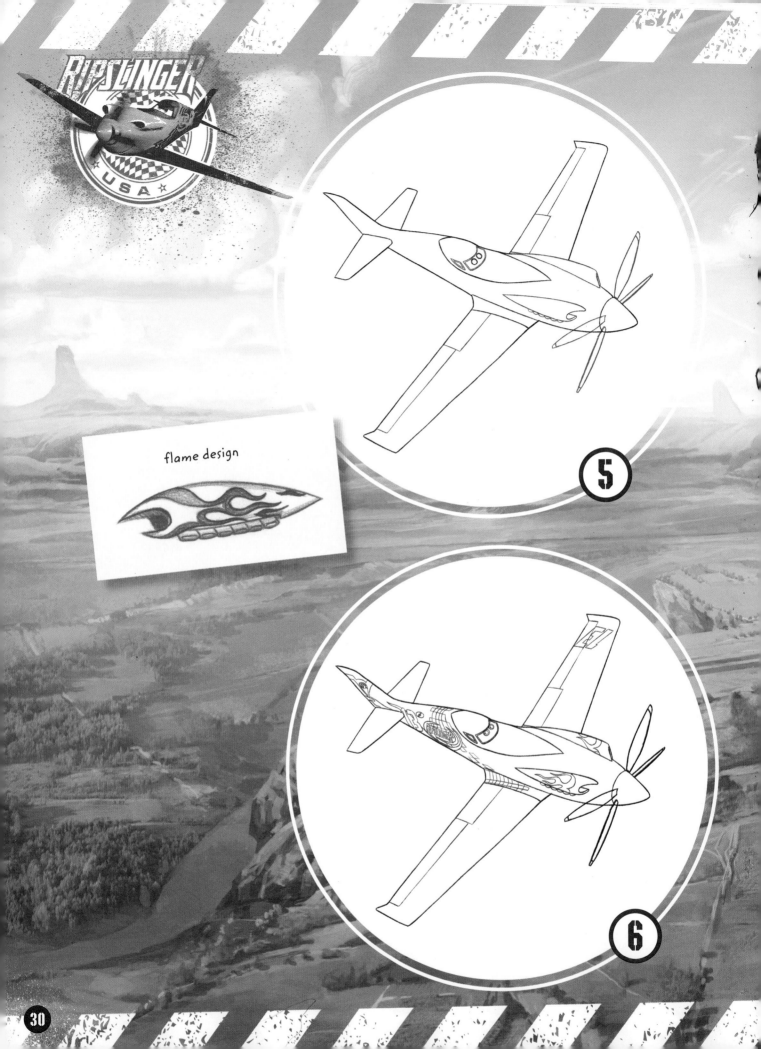

RIPSLINGER USA

flame design

⑤

⑥

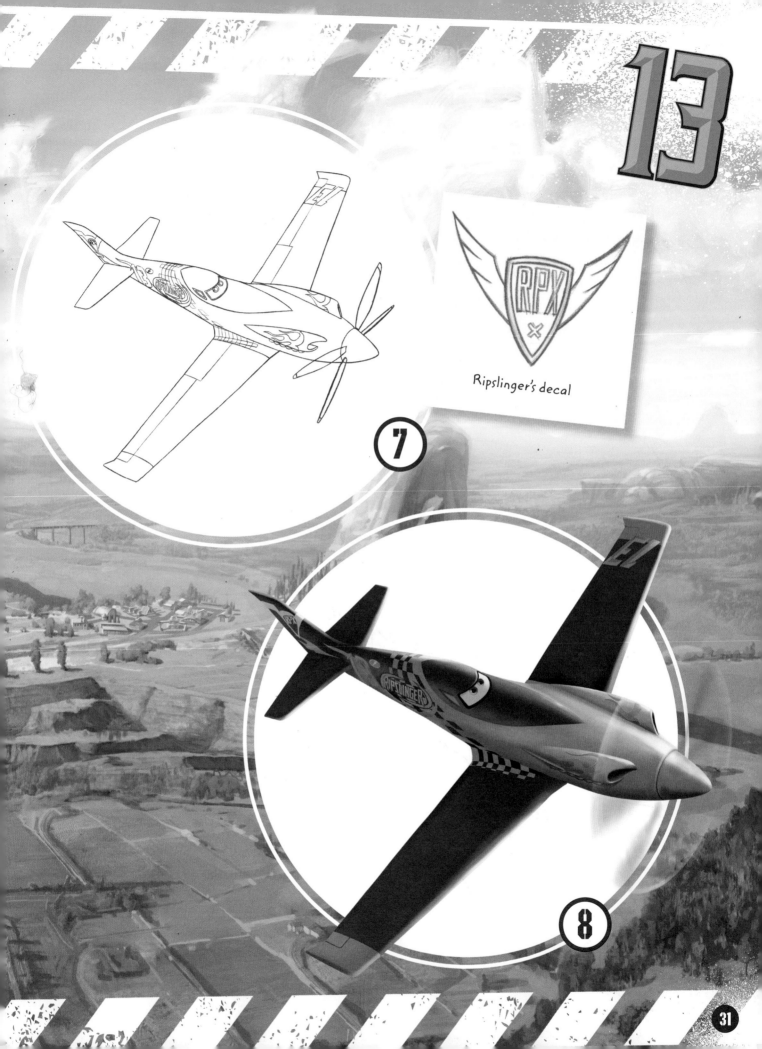

Ripslinger's decal

⑦

⑧

ISHANI

As the reigning Pan-Asian champion from India, Ishani is easy on the eyes, but ruthless in the skies. Thanks to her high-speed competitiveness and talent, she has more than a billion loyal fans—including one rookie racer who turns to her for guidance. Exotic and mysterious, Ishani is full of surprises, but she always has her eye on the prize.

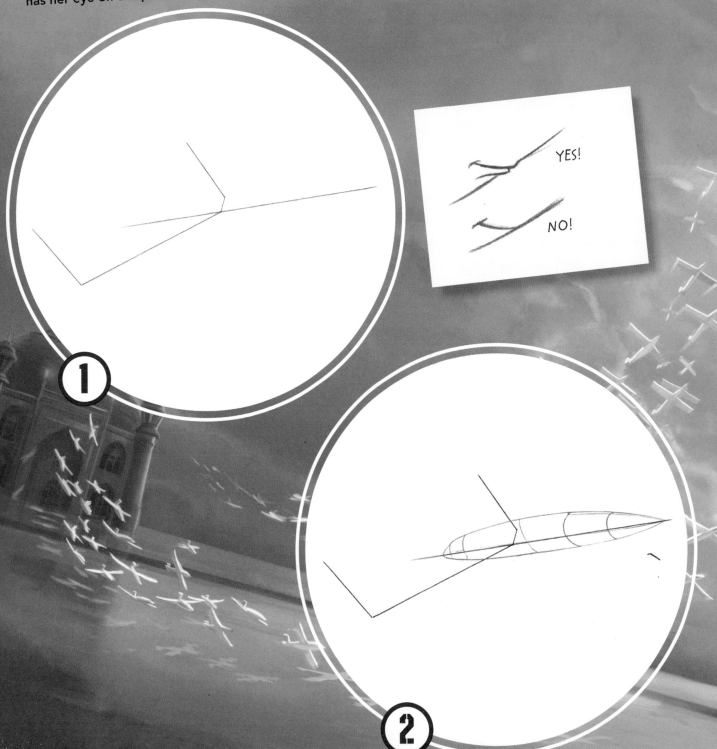

YES!

NO!

① ②

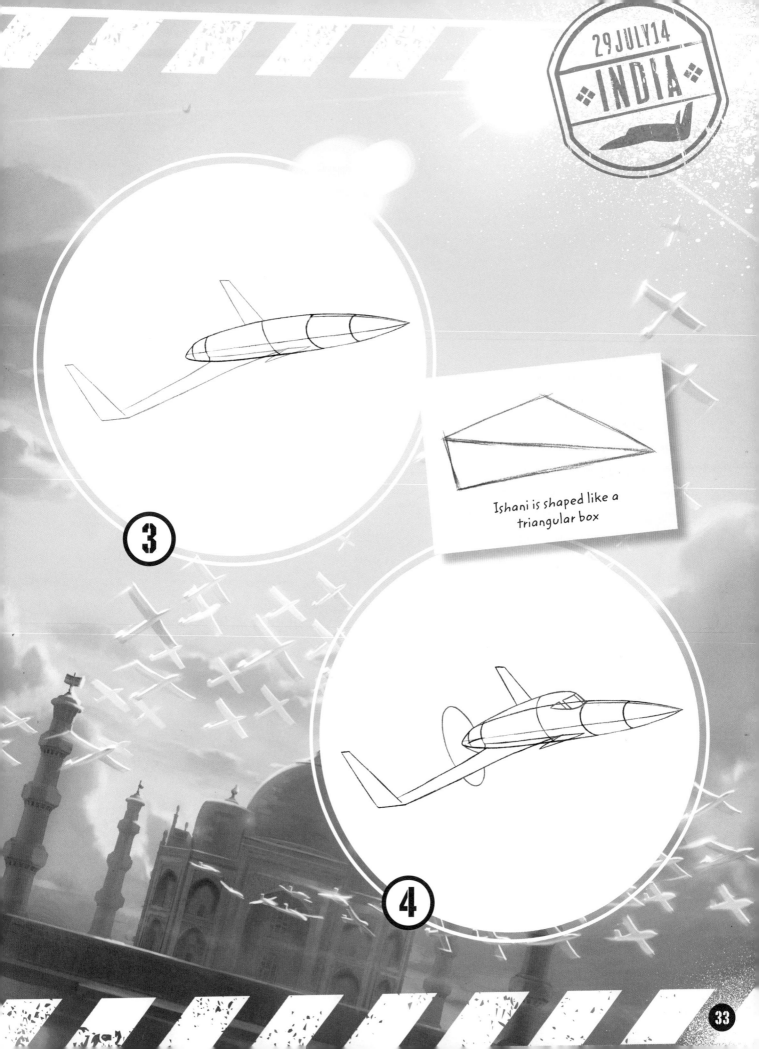

③

④

Ishani is shaped like a
triangular box

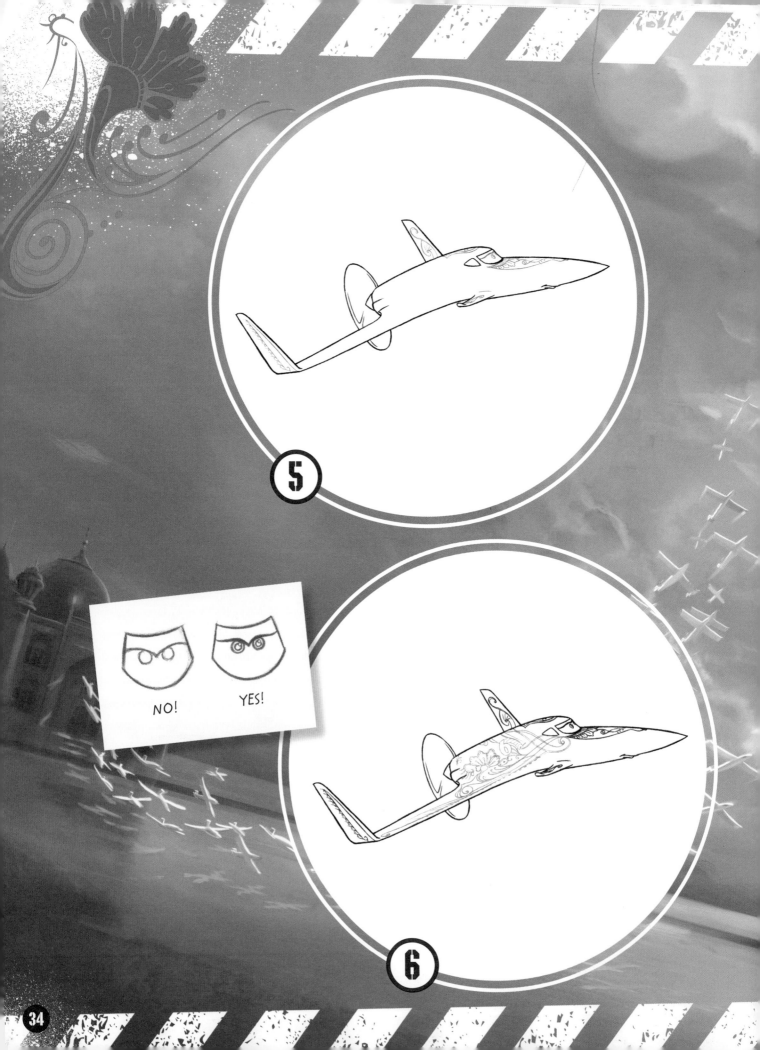

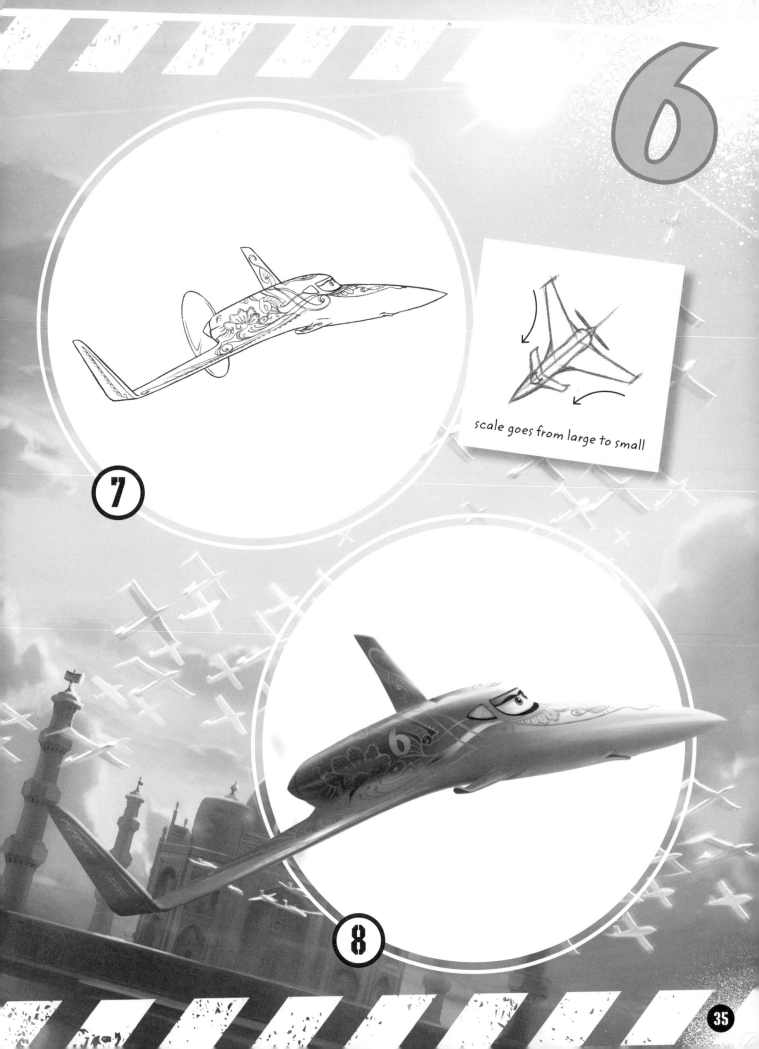

6

7

scale goes from large to small

8

NED & ZED

Team Ripslinger's henchmen Ned and Zed specialize in sabotage. Lacking the skills to outrace the competition, they simply eliminate it, propelling boss Ripslinger to victory every single time. These two troublemakers may not be the sharpest props in the hangar, but they have figured out how to ride the tailwinds of Ripslinger's fame.

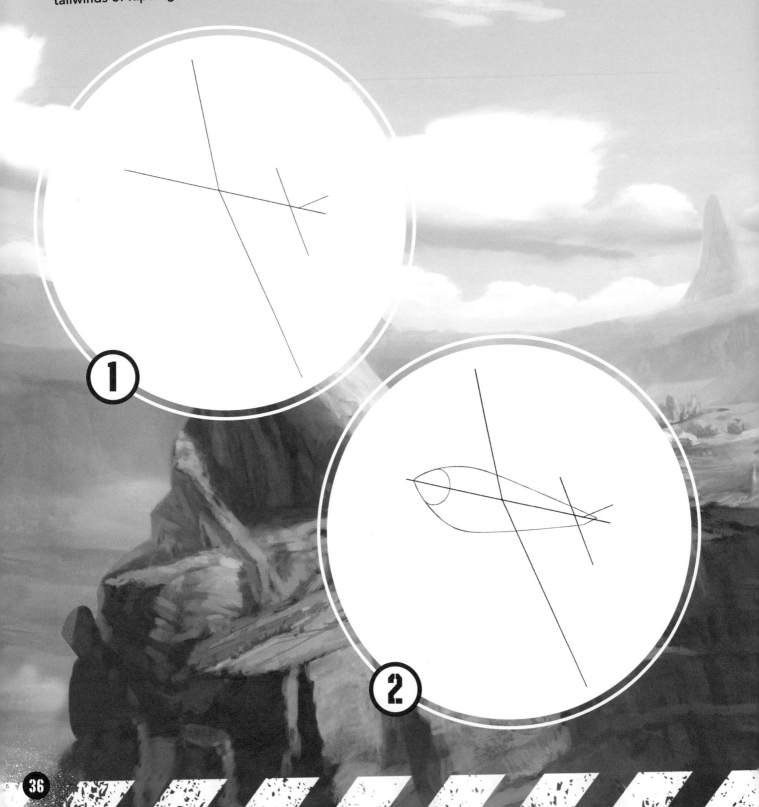

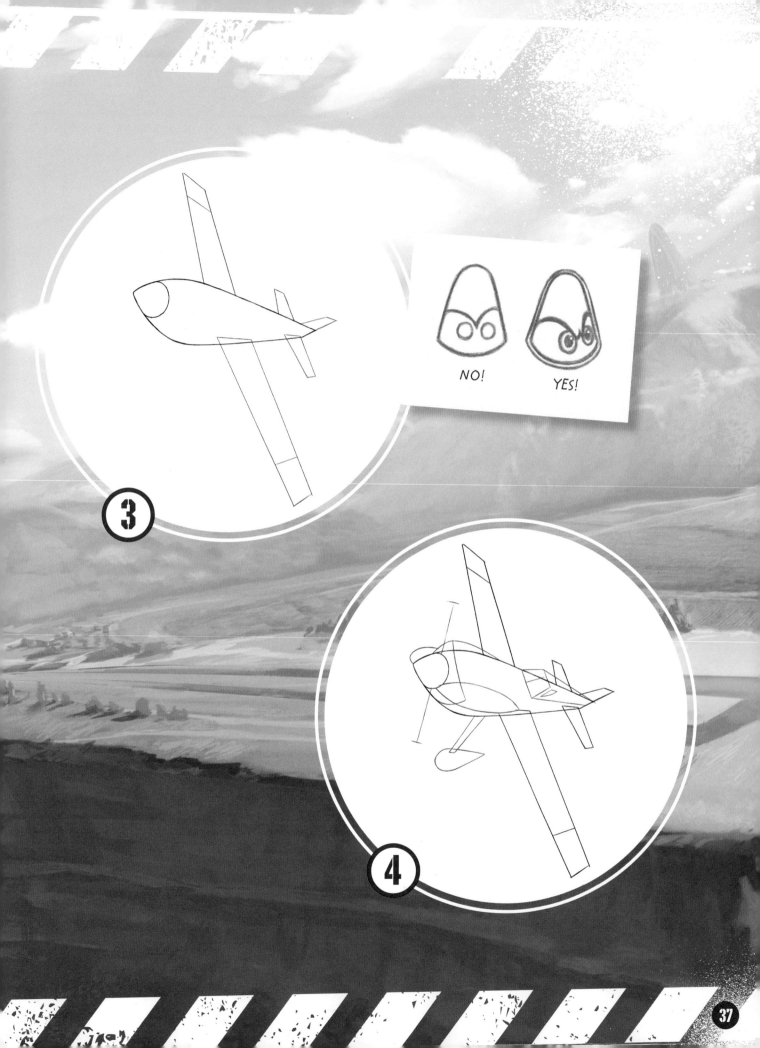

NO!   YES!

3

4

5

Follow the same steps to draw Zed!

His design has just three differences:
- wing has a "00" at the end
- tail has the letter "Z"
- body is white and wings are green

6

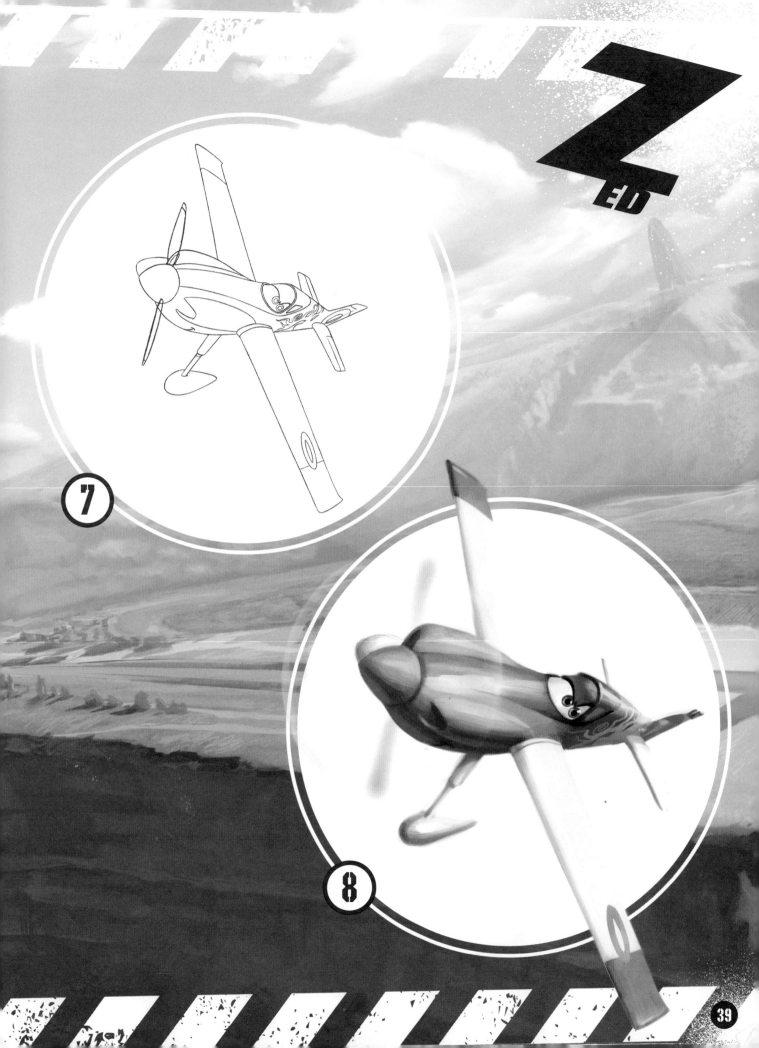

Z ED

7

8

ECHO & BRAVO

Armed with stellar instincts, incredible aerial abilities, and outstanding service records, Bravo and Echo are two of the Jolly Wrenches' top troops. These fighter jets happen to be avid air-racing fans too, and—like good, protective soldiers—they look out for Dusty, who has adopted their Jolly Wrenches insignia.

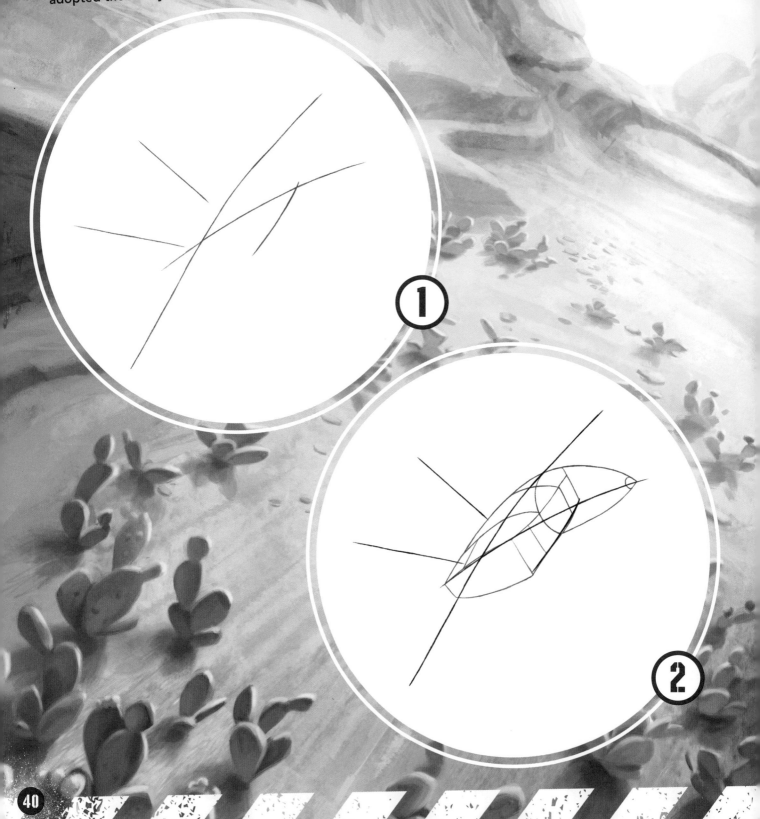

ECHO
J W 210

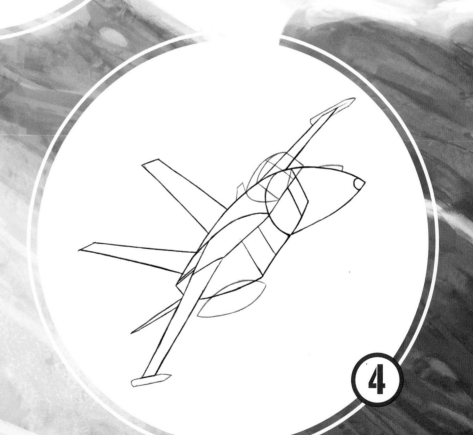

side decal

③

④

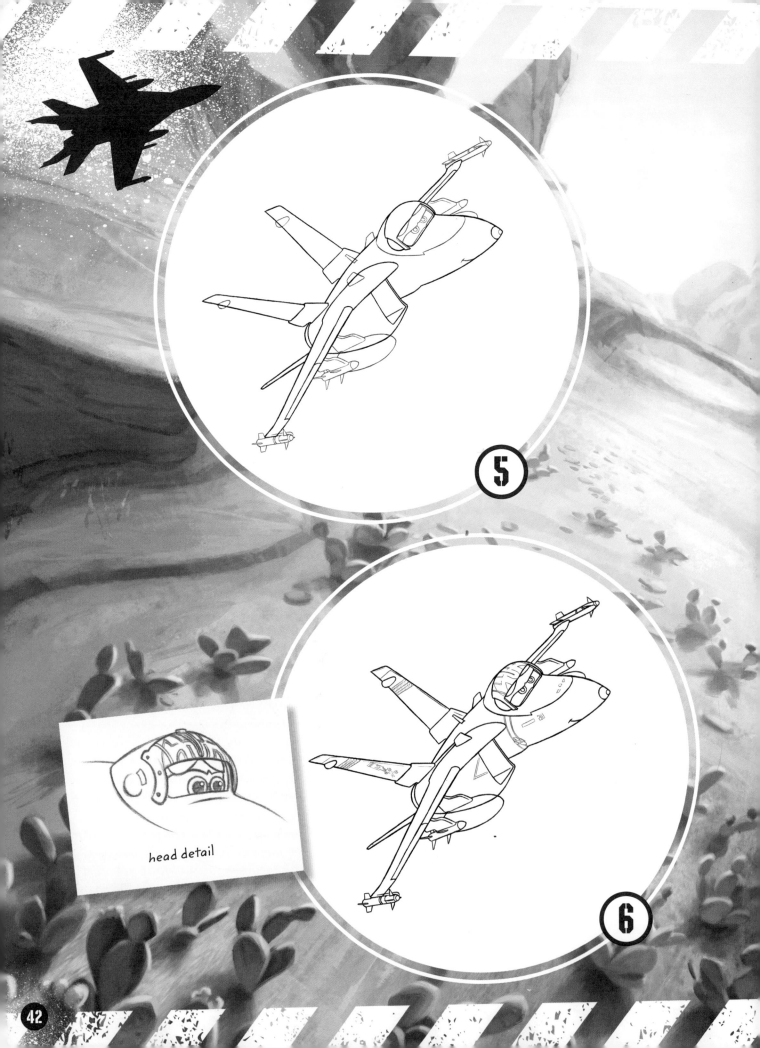

head detail

⑤

⑥

BRAVO
113
JW

⑦

Follow the same steps to draw Bravo!

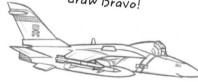

His design has just three differences:

- helmet has two lightning bolts down the middle
- head and tail have #113
- helmet is silver

⑧

ROCHELLE

Rochelle is a tough racer and the pride of the Great White North. Always confident and capable, she got her start running mail to small towns in Quebec, picking up home remedies for mechanical illnesses along the way. She also developed a knack for fast travel that ultimately inspired her to start air racing. Rochelle hasn't looked back since—despite persistent attention from charmer El Chupacabra, steadfast Rochelle is much too focused on winning the race!

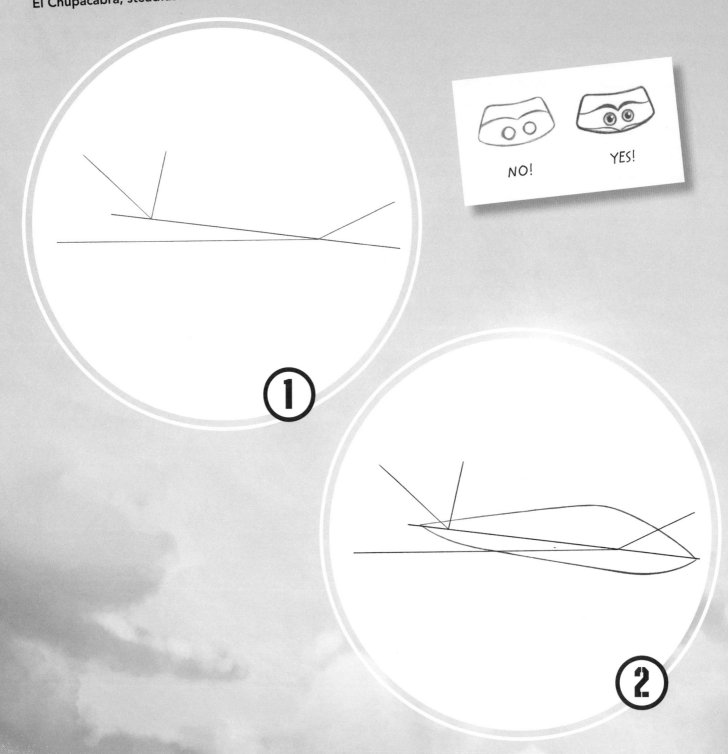

NO!   YES!

①

②

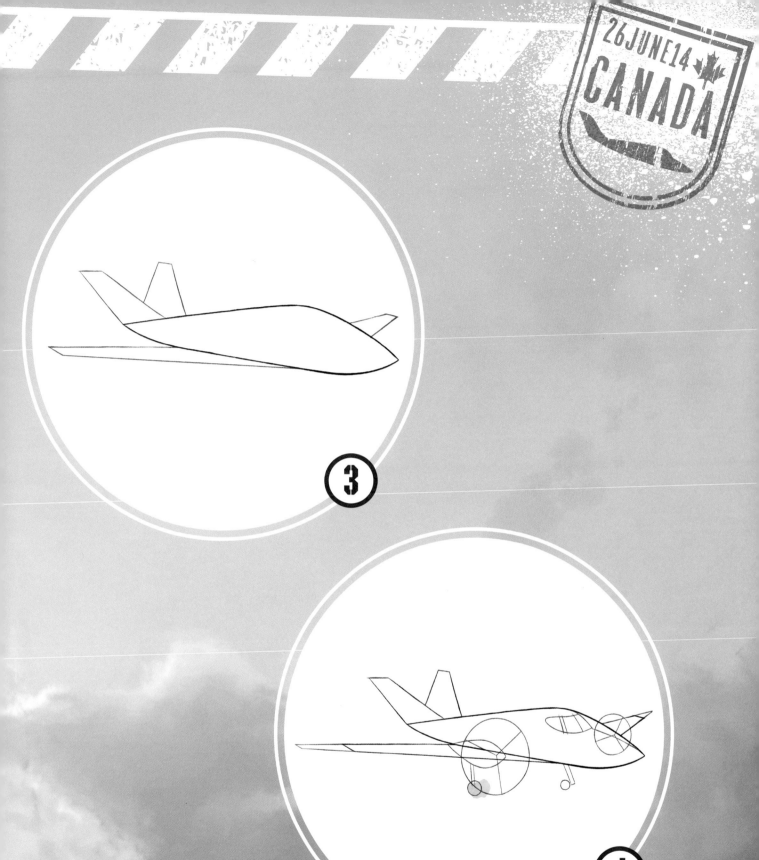

③

④

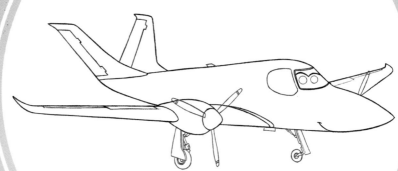

5

maple leaf decal because
she is from Canada

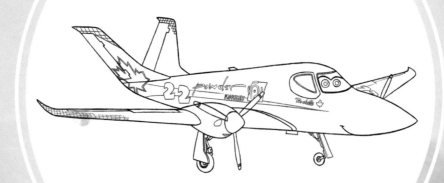

6

22

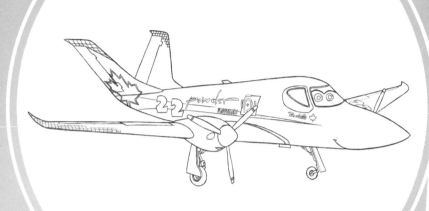

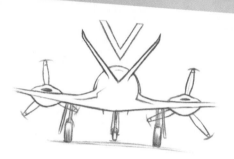

tail wings shaped like a "V"

7

8

47

BULLDOG

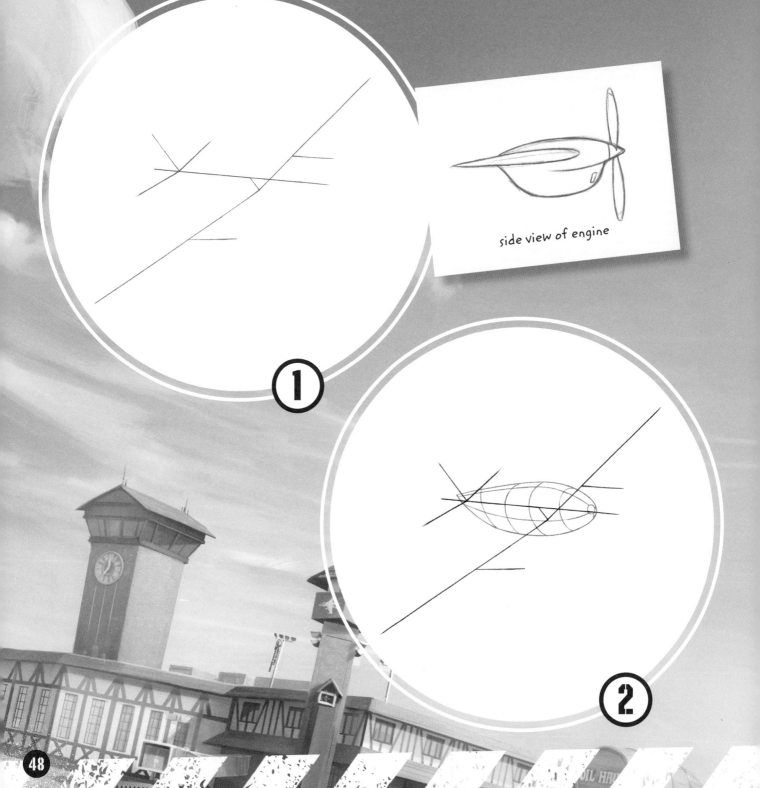

Bulldog has been racing longer than every other racer on the circuit. As the oldest and arguably wisest, he remembers a time before GPS, when real racers trusted compasses and navigated by the stars. According to Bulldog, racing boils down to just two qualities: good flying and sportsmanship. While the competition secretly wonders if Bulldog is past his prime, this old-timer continues to fly his way onto the leader board.

11

side view of engine

1

2

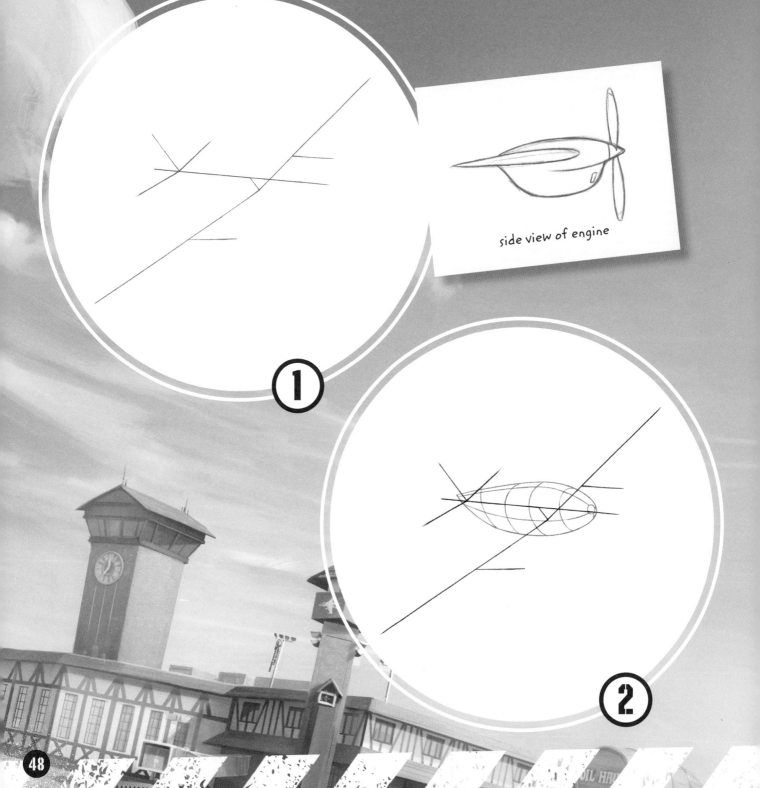

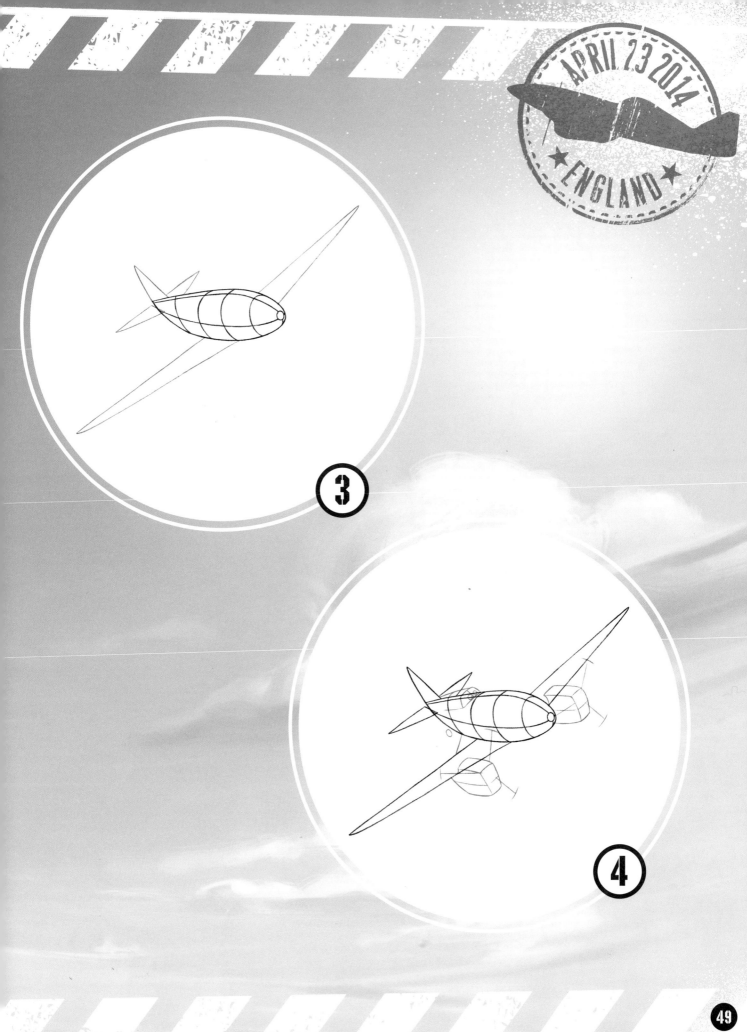

③

④

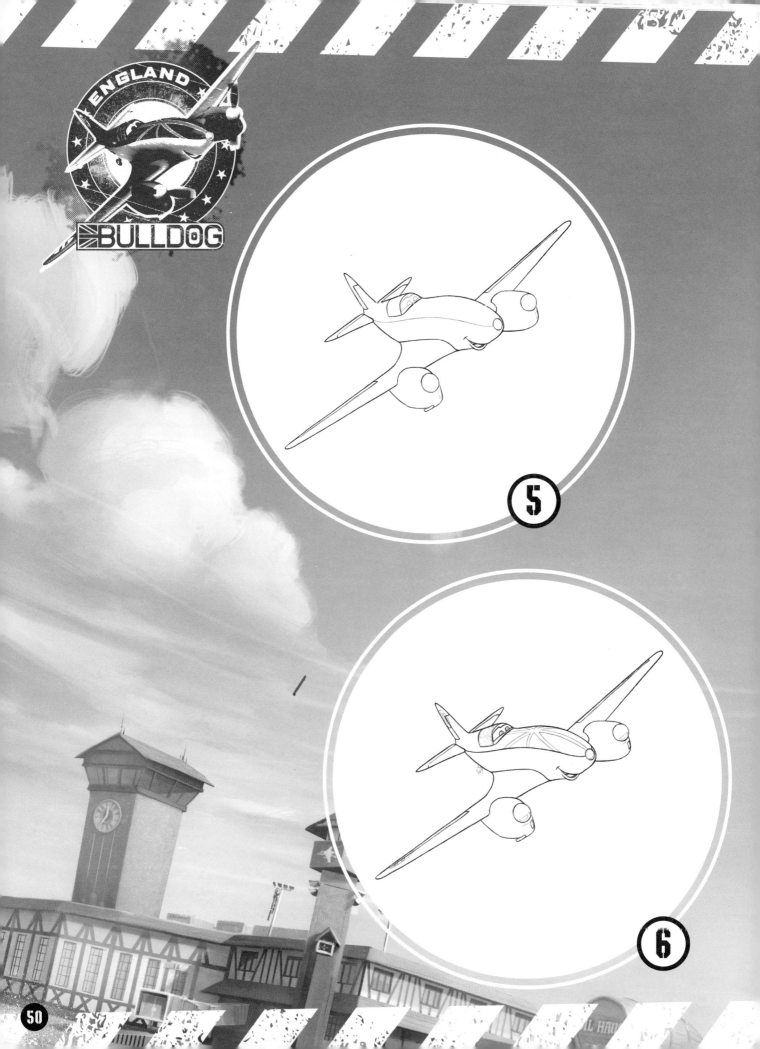

BULLDOG

⑤

⑥

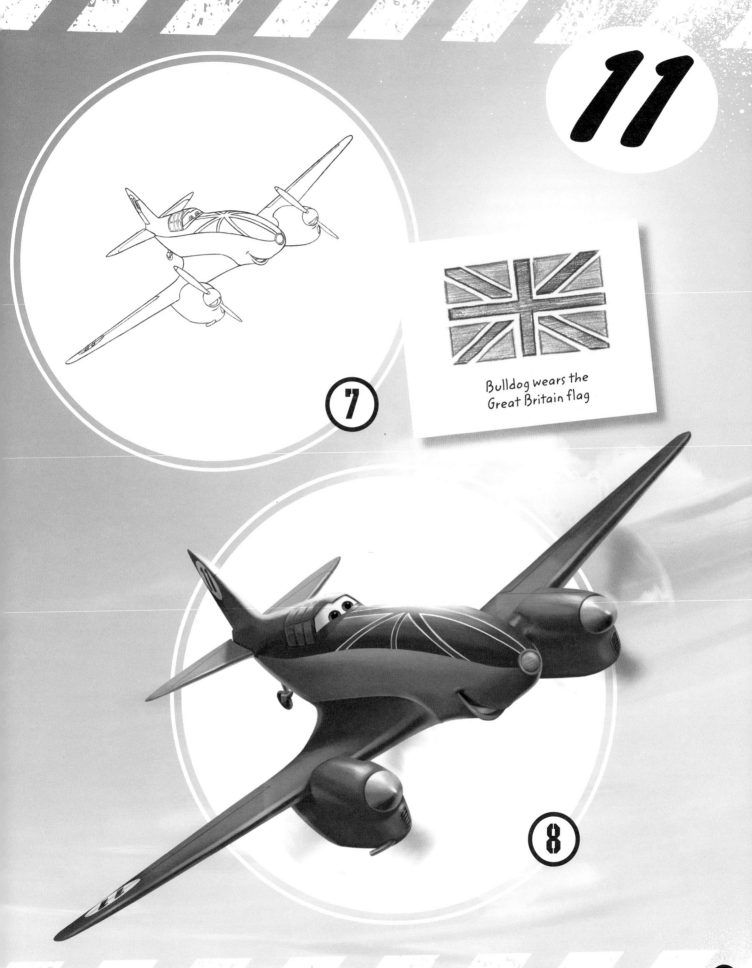

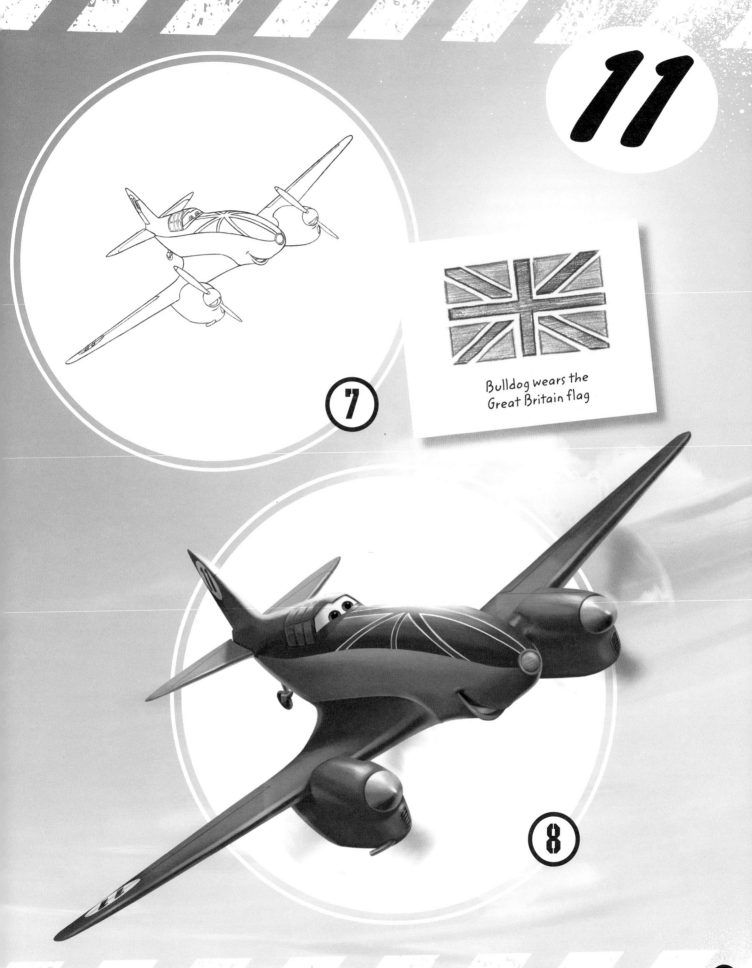

Bulldog wears the
Great Britain flag

7

8

11

LEADBOTTOM

Leadbottom is a puttering old biplane and a grumbling taskmaster—a real "tank-half-empty" kind of guy. As the owner of Vitaminamulch, a special yet stinky blend of vitamins, minerals, and mulch that works miracles when sprayed on crops, Leadbottom has no time for Dusty's far-fetched ambitions. For Leadbottom, it's work first and then...well, more work.

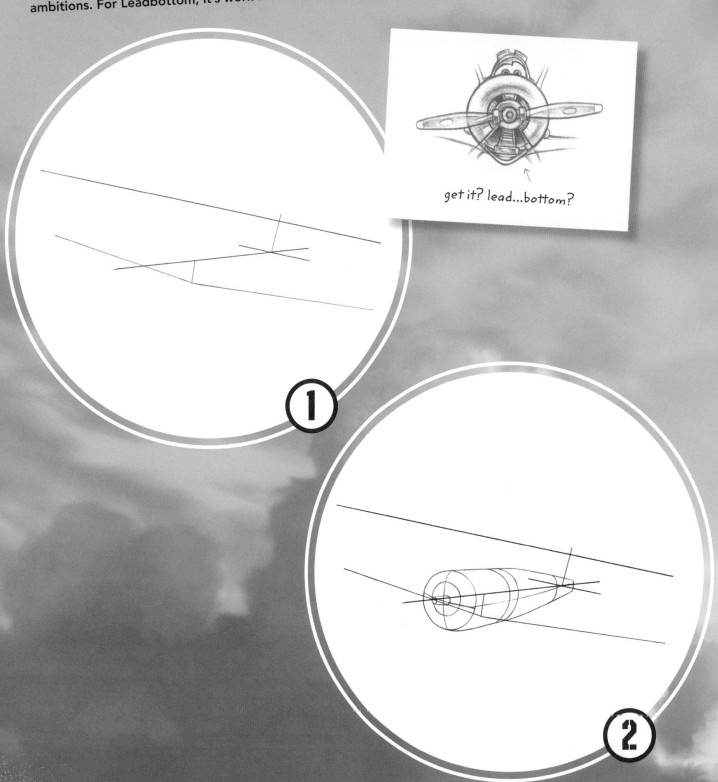

get it? lead...bottom?

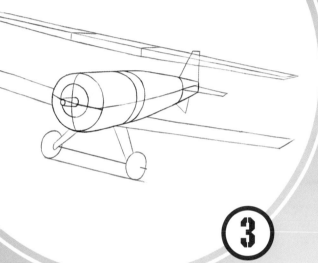

③

give him a pair of
pilot goggles!

④

5

6

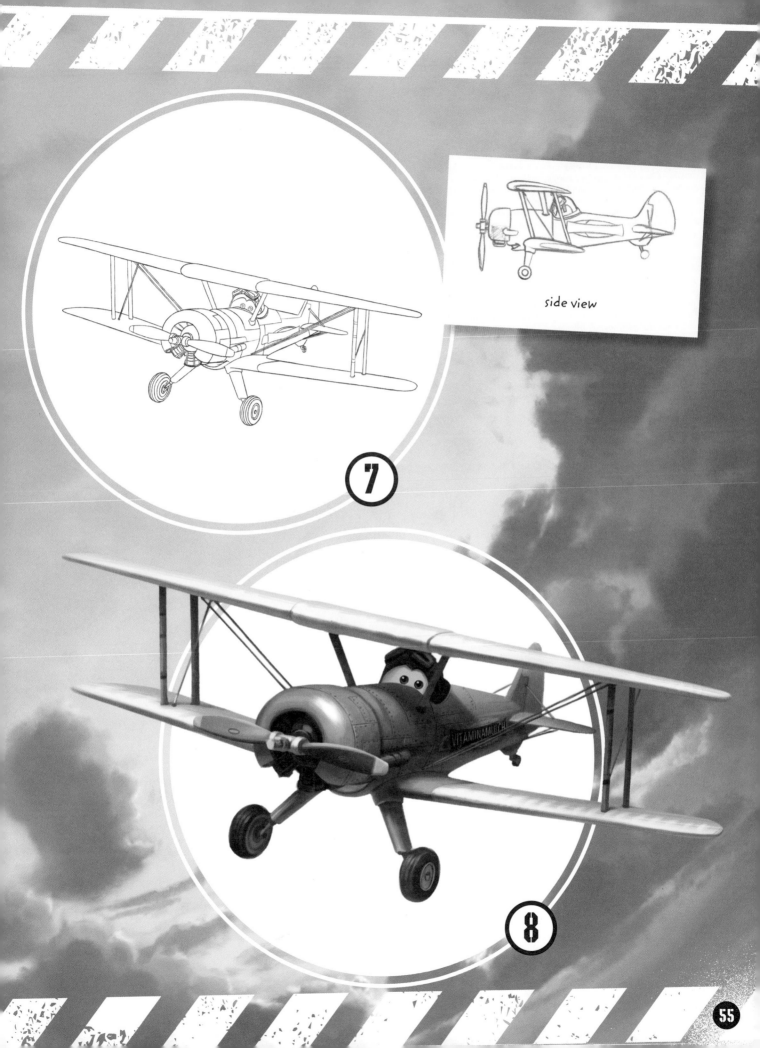

side view

⑦

⑧

CHUG

Fuel truck Chug is a guy's guy. He works hard as co-owner of Chug and Dottie's Fill 'n Fly service station—and he plays hard indulging in his own fuel from time to time. He has a big personality and is a bold supporter of Dusty's high-flying endeavors. He's not only Dusty's buddy, he's his first coach and biggest fan.

(1)

less detail:

do this when you draw him from a distance

more detail:

do this when you draw him up close

(2)

tires look like a pizza with eight slices

5

6

8   2

7   3

6   4

5

Chug's decal

7

8

DOTTiE

Dottie is a forklift who co-owns and operates Chug and Dottie's Fill 'n Fly service station. As Dusty's practical friend, Dottie tries to keep his high-flying hopes grounded in reality: Dusty isn't built to race, and chasing his dream is downright dangerous. No matter what he decides, however, Dottie will always have his back.

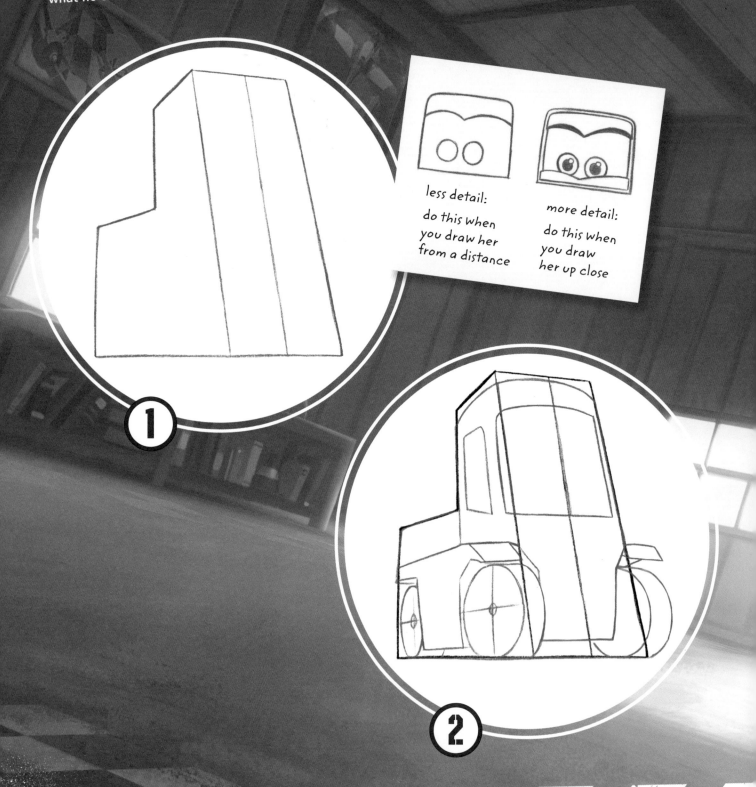

less detail:
do this when you draw her from a distance

more detail:
do this when you draw her up close

(3)

NO!

YES!

(4)

AEROFLEX
COMPOSITES

5

6

tool belt detail

7

8

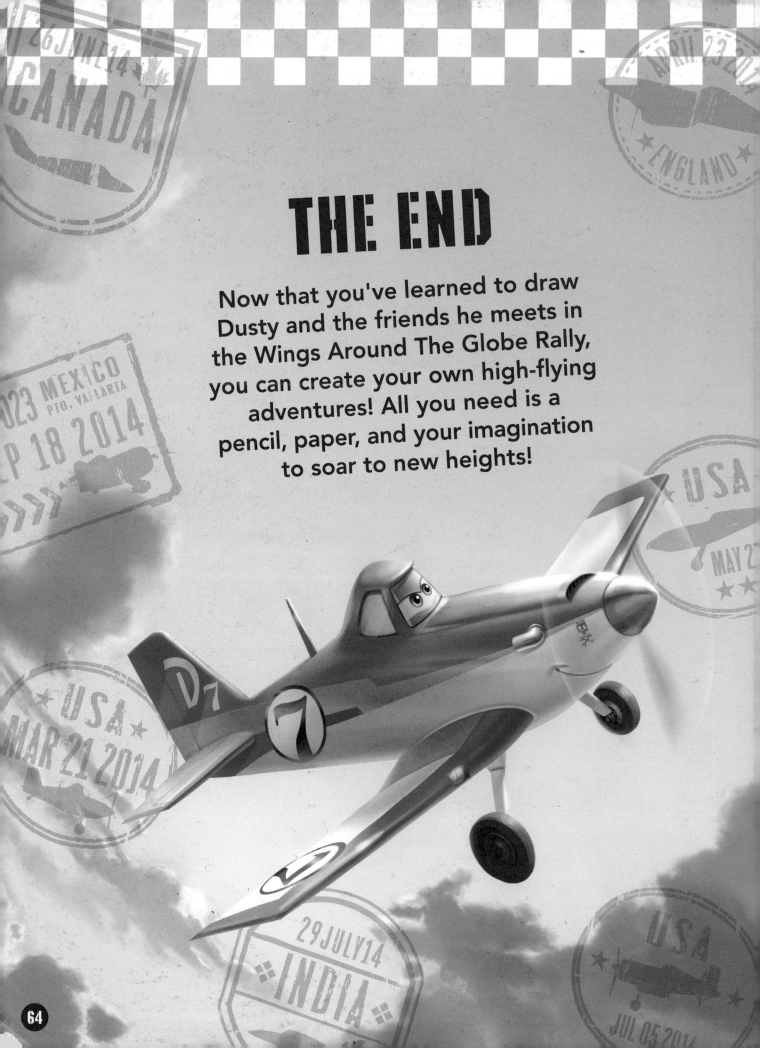

THE END

Now that you've learned to draw Dusty and the friends he meets in the Wings Around The Globe Rally, you can create your own high-flying adventures! All you need is a pencil, paper, and your imagination to soar to new heights!